insight text guide

Ross Walker

Nineteen Eighty-Four

George Orwell

First published in 2006, reprinted in 2010, 2015, 2016, 2017, 2018, 2019, 2020, 2021, 2025.

Insight Publications Pty Ltd
3/350 Charman Road
Cheltenham VIC 3192
Australia
Tel: +61 3 8571 4950
Email: books@insightpublications.com.au

www.insightpublications.com.au

National Library of Australia Cataloguing-in-Publication entry:

Walker, Ross, 1957–.
George Orwell's Nineteen Eighty-Four: text guide.
For secondary students.
ISBN 9781921088674
1. Orwell, George, 1903–1950. Nineteen Eighty-Four. I. Title
823.912

Other ISBNs:

9781925778816 (digital)

Cover design: The Modern Art Production Group

Printed by Markono Print Media Pte Ltd

contents

CHARACTER MAP

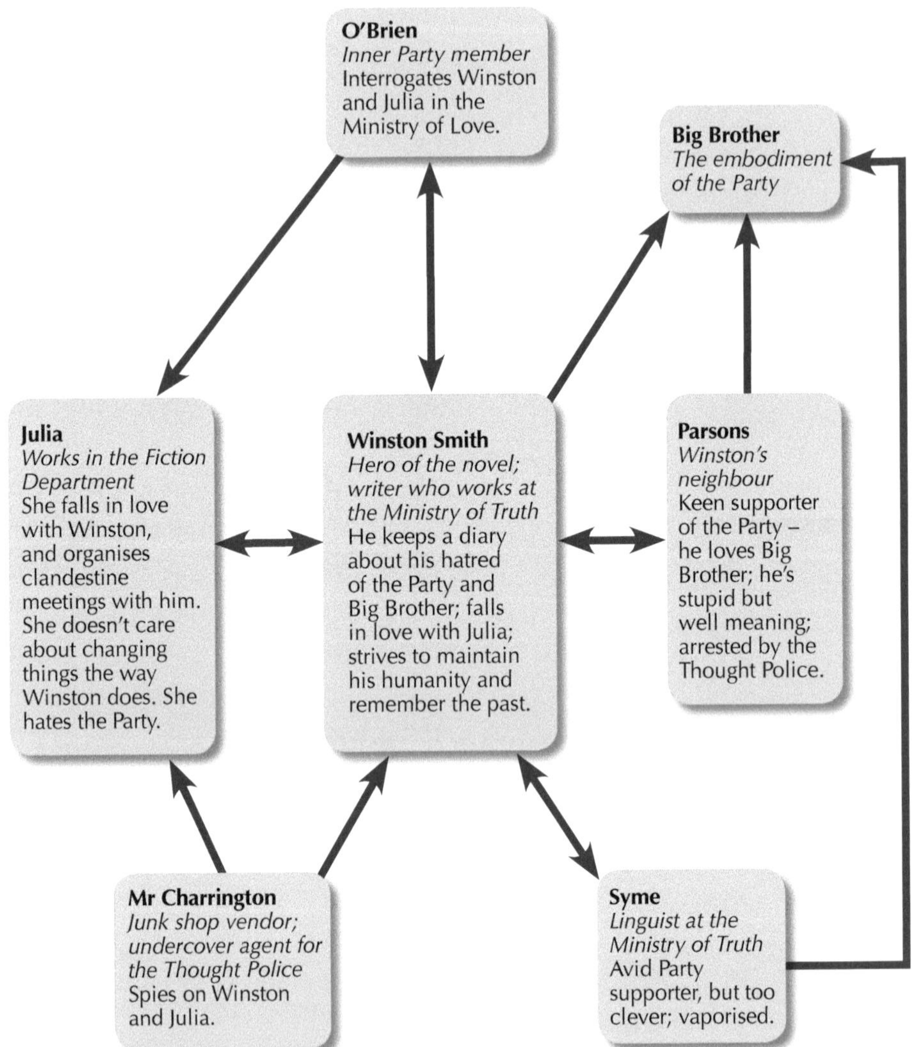

INTRODUCTION

George Orwell: a passionate man

George Orwell will always be remembered for his last novel, *Nineteen Eighty-Four*. Nearing the end of his life, he retreated to the Scottish island of Jura. There, battling against the ill health which plagued so much of his life, he worked furiously to finish the novel. The sense of urgency with which he worked testified to his sense of the book's importance. He meant for this work to stand as a timeless warning to all humanity of the evil of totalitarian tyranny. Totalitarian government can be defined as a centralised system of government in which a single party without opposition rules over political, economic, social and cultural life.

Orwell was indeed a 'political animal'. All his works bear witness to his preoccupation with social conditions and the social structures within which people live. He always maintained a strong sense of social justice and outrage against the evils inflicted on people by their rulers. Although his politics were decisively left of centre and although he called himself a socialist, he constantly pointed out weaknesses in socialism. That was typical of his nature, for perhaps more than anything else, he abhorred blind conformity to any philosophy or creed. He cherished the independence of mind that is threatened by slavish adherence to belief systems. *Nineteen Eighty-Four* reveals the truth that any political philosophy, whether of the Right or the Left, is capable of enslaving people when that philosophy is put into practice with the fanatical zeal that crushes fundamental human rights. Above all, the novel reveals Orwell to be a humanist, a man with a firm belief in both the dignity of humanity and the need to preserve it. Orwell was making no ideological distinction when he wrote in

1946 that 'politics itself is a mass of lies, evasions, folly, hatred, and schizophrenia' (Orwell 2000, p.357).

Orwell's biographer, Michael Shelden, notes that 'there is some reflection of [Orwell's] character in almost everything he wrote' (1991, p.355). Although *Nineteen Eighty-Four* describes a brutally bleak work, it reveals some of the most attractive aspects of its author's humanity: his unshakeable belief in the importance of the individual; his fierce intelligence; and his love of nature and of 'useless', but beautiful, objects to be found in junk shops.

BACKGROUND & CONTEXT

1948 becomes 1984

Orwell wrote this novel during the year 1948. Apparently, he obtained his futuristic date by transposing the final two digits of the year of writing. While the novel represents his vision of a nightmare totalitarian future, his setting of the city of London in the state of Oceania is largely based on post-war England. The descriptions of the physical conditions of the city mirror those of the country which had just recently emerged from the devastating war against Hitler's Germany. Orwell spent much of the war in London and he would have witnessed the daily German Blitz against that city. The London of 1984 exists under a rain of bombs and rockets, just like the actual London of the early 1940s. Although England won the war against Hitler, the peace was hard and austere. Recovery was slow: ruined buildings were everywhere, essential items were rationed and in Eastern Europe a new threat was emerging in the shape of Soviet Russia.

Stalinist Russia

During World War II, Britain, the United States and Australia joined with Russia to fight against Germany. At the end of the war, the United States had established its sphere of influence in Western Europe and Russia had control over Eastern Europe. The stage was set for a confrontation between these two ideologically opposed countries; the 'Cold War' had begun. The Western democracies, especially the United States, were deeply opposed to communism, the dominant ideology of the Russian regime. The goal of communist philosophy was to create a classless society in which capitalism was overthrown by a working-class revolution that would give ownership and control of wealth and property to a one-party state.

In 1946, during a visit to the United States the British wartime Prime Minister, Winston Churchill (1874–1965), declared that 'an Iron Curtain' had descended on Eastern Europe. He was referring to Soviet Russia's domination of Eastern Europe. The Russian dictator, Joseph Stalin (1879–1953), who ruled Russia from 1922 until his death in 1953, sought to expand Soviet influence in the East and throughout the rest of the world. He conducted a reign of terror inside Russia itself. His portrait looked down upon his people all over Russia. Much like the portrait of Big Brother himself, it was a ubiquitous image of his power and menace. Stalin was responsible for the deaths of millions inside Russia; any hint of dissent could be deadly. He imposed a grim uniformity on Russia and the satellite countries of Eastern Europe, quite similar to that which Orwell depicts in Oceania. He made creative art and literature impossible; the only art or literature permissible was that which extolled the glories and achievements of the state. Everything had to be subjugated to the will of the state and its ruler. A sense of individuality – 'ownlife' in Newspeak – was considered a crime. In *Nineteen Eighty-Four*, O'Brien explains that no works of literature are written by individuals. In Stalinist Russia, creative artists such as the writers Boris Pasternak and Alexander Solzhenitsyn, and composers such as Sergei Prokofiev and Dmitri Shostakovich, were accused of producing 'anti-Soviet' works.

This is not to imply that Orwell necessarily intended Big Brother to represent Stalin. Big Brother, after all, is not an actual person. He represents the spirit of extremist government of any complexion. The repression, terror and murder of the Third Reich of Adolf Hitler (1889–1945), only recently defeated when

Orwell wrote the novel, must have been in the author's mind as he wrote. The mass hysteria of the public rallies organised by the Party bring to mind Hitler's huge Nazi Party rallies. Nazism (German 'National Socialism') was the political ideology founded by Hitler. It was characterised by fanatical nationalism, ruthless suppression of all domestic opposition and especially fierce anti-Semitism which ultimately resulted in the extermination of six million European Jews. (Emmanuel Goldstein, the scapegoat for all ills in Oceania is Jewish. Anti-Semitism was also a prominent feature of Stalin's regime.)

Yet Big Brother has the godlike stature which was accorded to Stalin. In addition many aspects of the Party's rule in Oceania mirror Stalinist Russia, for example, the shortage and the inferior quality of vital goods available, the constant surveillance of the citizens, the torture chambers where dissidents were sent for 're-education' and the falsification of history to create a world in which the Party is always right. The Soviet regime incarcerated dissidents (those who publicly criticised the regime) in psychiatric hospitals – just as dissidents such as Winston Smith in Orwell's novel were judged to be insane. But Big Brother has come to be a symbol of the kind of power which dictators like Stalin imposed upon their people. Orwell would have been surprised indeed to learn that these days his creation is often known only as the title of a popular reality TV program.

The prescience (capacity to predict future events) of Orwell's novel is remarkable. Orwell understood acutely the mentality behind totalitarian government – so much so that many examples in recent history mirror the abuses of the regime of Big Brother. During the 'Cultural Revolution' of Mao Zedong's China, which took place from 1965 to 1968, Mao (1893–1976) had semi-divine status and schools in China taught little beside the precepts of *The Little Red Book,* which he wrote. The Cultural

Revolution was a political and cultural reform movement that aimed to revolutionise political opinion and behaviour. More recently, the same semi-divine status has been attained by Kim Jong-il, the leader of North Korea, the most rigidly communist state in the world today. Orwell depicted, too, the widespread economic failure of communism. In *Nineteen Eighty-Four*, the population is constantly bombarded with bogus statistics designed to prove that the standard of living is constantly rising, while the majority of people live lives of poverty and deprivation.

We could describe the totalitarianism of the Party as a mindset, just as religious fundamentalism is a mindset. That is, what the fundamentalist actually believes eventually becomes a matter of only secondary importance. What is considered most important is that no one should think differently – to have a dissenting view is 'thoughtcrime'. Big Brother lives on in the leaders of the Taliban in Afghanistan, or the mullahs of Iran. He lives in the terrorists who seek to impose their power on those of a different ideology and who commit their atrocities in the name of God. The sadistic cruelty of their acts bears out the truth of O'Brien's admission that the Party seeks power for its own sake, rather than for any higher purpose.

At the same time, perhaps there are some grounds for greater optimism than Orwell might have felt when he ended his novel with the depressing announcement that Winston 'had won the victory over himself' since he finally 'loved Big Brother' (p.311). As we look around the world and see the decline of communism, there may be reason to believe in Winston's hope that 'the spirit of Man' can win against the forces that strive to crush it. The liberalisation of the Gorbachev era in Russia, culminating in the demolition of the Berlin Wall, which separated the Soviet bloc from the Western bloc, and the triumph of Lech Wałęsa's *Solidarność* (Solidarity) movement in Poland, bear witness to the strength of that spirit.

Orwell's *Animal Farm*

To better understand *Nineteen Eighty-Four,* it is important to read Orwell's short fable *Animal Farm*. It was published in 1944, towards the end of World War II. Orwell's criticism of Russian communism, especially of the Soviet leader, Joseph Stalin (who was pilloried in the figure of the pig Napoleon) made it hard for Orwell to find a publisher for the novel. As Russia was then fighting against Hitler alongside the Western Allies, many people considered it bad policy to risk offending Stalin. Some of the central themes of *Nineteen Eighty-Four* are present in the earlier novel: the oppression of the majority of the people by an unscrupulous ruling elite, the seeking of power for its own sake, the alteration of history and the manipulation of language as tools of social control. Whereas the writing in *Animal Farm* is marked by a certain lightness of touch, *Nineteen Eighty-Four* is thoroughly overlaid with a sense of darkness and doom. The alliance between Stalinist Russia and the Western powers, especially the United States, had turned into the Cold War by the time Orwell began his last work. This meant that he had no further difficulty in finding a publisher for it. Yet he undoubtedly would not have wished his work to be used as propaganda by those of any political persuasion. Rather, Orwell's writing strikes a blow for freedom and warns against political excesses of any complexion.

GENRE, STRUCTURE & STYLE

Genre

This novel is hard to classify. Some readers describe it as a work of science fiction. It has elements of this, with its futuristic setting and its vision of a nightmare world of telescreens, mind control and Newspeak. Others have seen the novel as a polemic, a tract opposing totalitarianism. It is true that parts of the novel give credibility to this view, such as the interpolated (inserted into the text) extract from 'Goldstein's book'. A number of the characters, too, have been constructed to represent certain ideological positions, rather than as individuals in their own right, such as O'Brien; Parsons, the Party enthusiast; and Syme, the linguist at the Ministry of Truth. After all, Orwell was fond of theorising and wrote much non-fiction that argues a point of view.

But to classify the book as primarily a work of propaganda, a didactic work, is to ignore its creative and imaginative elements. Where propaganda begins, art stops, as Orwell certainly knew. It is important to remember that in *Nineteen Eighty-Four* we are dealing with the work of a creative artist. So much of Orwell's own humanity is in the novel: his wry observation of human behaviour and other personal touches are everywhere. The characters of Winston and Julia are fully realised as individuals in their own right, and the love relationship between them, which lies at the heart of the novel, is depicted with imagination and warmth.

Structure

The narrative of the novel, for the most part, moves forward chronologically, with periodic flashbacks in which fragments of Winston's past are recalled. These flashbacks show Winston trying to make sense of his present life by placing it into the wider context which the Party has set out to eradicate. The narrative is interrupted by the lengthy insertion of the extract from Goldstein's book, which can be read as Orwell's theoretical exposition and denunciation of totalitarian government. Orwell's publishers attempted to get him to omit this section of the novel, arguing – with some justification, I think – that it interrupts the novel's central narrative. At the end of the novel is another insertion, a kind of addendum to the text, in which the narrator (whose views seem to represent those of Orwell himself) outlines the 'principles of Newspeak' (p.312). Orwell's editors urged him to omit this, too. While some might find this addendum anti-climactic following the dramatic conclusion to the story itself, others could argue that it serves as a further indictment of the mentality of dictators and is therefore thoroughly in keeping with the spirit of the novel.

The novel is structured to create maximum dramatic impact by building up suspense and tension. We know that Winston is placing himself in dire danger at a number of key moments in the story: firstly, when he opens his notebook and begins to write his private thoughts; then when he meets Julia and begins their sexual relationship; and when he seeks out and meets O'Brien. There is a sense of terrible inevitability about what then follows: the arrest and torture of both Winston and Julia, and Winston's decline to the point where he has 'won the victory over himself' and therefore 'loved Big Brother' (p.311).

Style

In a poem spoken at the end of the German playwright Bertolt Brecht's play about Hitler and the Nazis, *The Resistible Rise of Arturo Ui* (1941), the playwright invites his viewers to be aware of 'the horror at the heart of farce'. Orwell does likewise in *Nineteen Eighty-Four*. In doing so, he brings into play his sharp sense of the ridiculous. Some of Orwell's critics have claimed that his work lacks humour; however, this is an unjust charge. Black comedy is integral to Orwell's writing in this novel. His tone is often darkly sardonic, or mocking; he is a master of mockery, which can be a potent weapon against the ills and stupidities of humans. Orwell reveals the glaring gap between the rhetoric of the Party and its rulers, and the reality of conditions in Oceania. Everything has the label 'Victory' attached to it: Victory Gin, Victory Square, Victory Mansions, Victory Coffee, Victory Cigarettes. What an incongruous word to apply to any aspect of life in Oceania, yet so typical of the lies and fantasies of dictators. There is, too, Orwell's mockery of the language devised by the Party, with its ugly, staccato compound words such as 'speakwrite' or 'thoughtcrime'. Or again, his mockery of Parsons and Syme, party hacks and drones who grovel before their rulers with revolting sycophancy. He mocks anyone who takes himself too seriously – as totalitarian rulers always do. Who could forget, for example, O'Brien's remark that Winston's mind 'resembles my own mind except that you happen to be insane' (p.271). This comment is made by a man of 'lunatic enthusiasm' (p.268), whose every word betokens madness.

Orwell often fuses the ridiculous and the repulsive, as in his descriptions of the 'beetle-like' people who inhabit London under Ingsoc (p.118). His ability to enable his reader to *see* is often masterful, as he does when he describes the 'little Rumpelstiltskin figure' (p.188) spewing forth his venom during Hate Week – a truly representative image of twentieth-century political extremism. To create such images, Orwell uses highly connotative, enormously vital language, appropriate indeed for an author who railed against the language of 'Newspeak', stripped as it was of all emotive or aesthetic power.

None of this is to deny that the novel's tone is usually very dark. Orwell is writing about dreadful events, dreadful injustice and dreadful suffering. Yet it is a mark of his humanity and spirit that he is still able to leaven the heavy dough with his sense of irony and the absurd. Reading this novel, it is still possible to imagine Orwell as he was often observed, walking around with a wry smile on his face, as if amused by a private joke.

CHAPTER-BY-CHAPTER ANALYSIS

Part I (pp.3–107)

I (pp.3–22)

Summary: *Orwell's introduction to the world of Oceania. Winston begins to write in his notebook.*

The opening to the novel is disquieting. The detail of the clocks 'striking thirteen' ominously tells us that something is wrong; it is the kind of detail we might find in a work of science fiction. The pairing of the words 'bright' and 'cold' is unsettling, too, as the second undermines the positive connotations of the first. In a highly concentrated way, Orwell introduces us to the London of 1984. The impression is one of overpowering ugliness: decrepit and decaying buildings and houses, bad smells and even bad weather. The appearance of the city is caught exactly in the phrase, 'there seemed to be no colour in anything' (p.4). Over this scene looms the ubiquitous image of Big Brother, along with the caption 'BIG BROTHER IS WATCHING YOU'. It is a menacing image, designed to threaten and intimidate; as we will see, it is a symbol of the Party's control over its people.

This is a world of slogans – 'WAR IS PEACE', 'FREEDOM IS SLAVERY', 'IGNORANCE IS STRENGTH' (p.6). These are the slogans of a disordered world in which the incongruous is normal. It is a bureaucratic world of multiple ministries, each of which deals with the opposite of its official title. The Ministry of Love, the building with no windows, is the most terrifying of all.

Our view of Oceania is filtered through the perspective of Orwell's hero, Winston Smith. We are immediately invited to sympathise with this man. We are shown his constant suffering and discomfort – he is plagued with physical ailments – as well as his admirable desire to somehow maintain his dignity as an individual in the face of apparently insurmountable odds. This desire emerges when he begins to keep a personal diary. This highly dangerous act could be punished by death. It is significant that the book in which he chooses to write is 'a peculiarly beautiful book', an old book with 'smooth creamy paper' (p.8). For the first time, we see Winston's strong sense of beauty and his need to counteract the ugliness surrounding him.

Winston's first diary entry (pp.10–11) recounts a violent scene from a war film he has seen the previous night. We can see through his description of the audience's delight at the predicament of the drowning man that the sensitivities of the people in this society have been deadened; their responses are so warped that they take sadistic pleasure in the sufferings of others. Winston himself appears untroubled by the scene he has viewed, describing it in a matter-of-fact way and even taking pleasure in the 'wonderful shot of a child's arm going up up up right up into the air' as his boat is blown to matchwood (p.10).

But the most interesting aspect of his observations is his description of the 'middleaged woman' attempting to shelter her child (p.10). While he writes this down 'a totally different memory had clarified itself in his mind' (p.11). Later we learn that this is his childhood memory of his own mother sheltering his baby sister, a recurring and deeply significant memory for Winston.

For the first time, we are introduced to the other two main characters of the novel: Julia, who works in the Fiction Department, and O'Brien, a member of the 'Inner Party'. Julia is not named, but we later recognise that Orwell is describing her here. Winston dislikes her because of the atmosphere of clean outdoor living that attaches to her; later, we see that this is her disguise. Orwell gives greater attention to O'Brien here: we are made aware that Winston is 'deeply drawn to him' (p.13), although the reason for this is never entirely clarified. O'Brien is described as possessing apparently contradictory characteristics: his face is 'coarse' and 'brutal' but also 'humorous' (p.12); and he has an 'urbane manner' but 'a prizefighter's physique' (p.13). It becomes clear that Winston, suffering in his 'locked loneliness' (p.20), hopes to find in O'Brien a kindred spirit, an ally.

The chapter contains a substantial description of the 'Two Minutes Hate', a regular ritual organised by the Party. The focus of hate is always Emmanuel Goldstein, the commander of 'the Brotherhood', a secret organisation committed to the overthrow of the state. He is the unsighted and absent enemy who is made the scapegoat for all the society's ills. His Jewish identity brings to mind the scapegoating of Jewish people in both Hitler's Germany and Stalin's Russia. Goldstein's image appears on the telescreens so that people can revile him during the frenzied outpouring of negative emotion which is the Two Minutes Hate. At the end it is replaced by the image of Big Brother, an image designed to reassure and relieve. The Party's tactic here is a common one, used to varying degrees by governments both totalitarian and democratic: they create a sense of fear and menace, and then make the people feel dependent on the state by offering to protect them from these dangers. The Party presents Big Brother as a semi-divine figure, indeed, a substitute for God, as the behaviour of one woman attests, as she utters a prayer when she sees his face (p.18).

The chapter ends with Winston's act of ultimate 'thoughtcrime', as he writes 'DOWN WITH BIG BROTHER' over and over again in his notebook. Fatalistically, he accepts that this act will be the ruin of him, but he does it all the same. There is immense relief for him in committing this act of sedition. Perhaps, unconsciously, he even wishes to be caught in order to no longer feel so alone. Whatever the truth, the chapter ends on a distinctly ominous note. Winston is like the hero of a Greek tragedy, whose ultimate fate is inevitable from the beginning.

Q Follow the description of Winston throughout this chapter. How is Winston both ordinary and unusual?

Q How does this chapter prepare us for what is to come later in the novel?

II (pp.22–31)

Summary: *The Parsons are introduced. The concepts of Newspeak and doublethink are also introduced.*

The chapter opens with a blackly comic scene, as Winston goes into the flat of his neighbours, the Parsons, in order to fix a blocked drain. Their home is a shrine to the Party and the fanatical zeal of their children illustrates the fact that 'nearly all children ... were horrible' at this time (p.26). The Parsons children are indeed terrors, fiercely accusing Winston of being a 'traitor' and a 'thought-criminal' and attacking him with a bullet from a catapult. The children have obviously taken a terrible toll on their mother; clearly, they are in control and she is reduced to a 'helpless fright' when confronted with their behaviour. We can conclude that the Party is indoctrinating the youngest and most impressionable members of society. The description of the Party's activities for the children reads like the program of activities of the 'Hitler Youth' in Nazi Germany. (The 'Hitler Youth' was an organisation designed to instil in German youth a sense of patriotism and devotion to Hitler himself. It emphasised healthy outdoor activities and physical fitness.)

Though Mr Parsons himself is not at home when Winston visits, the overpowering smell of his sweat dominates the flat. It is no accident that Orwell introduces him in such an unflattering way.

Parsons is the embodiment of the type of person Orwell himself despised: a person 'of paralysing stupidity, a mass of imbecile enthusiasms' (p.24), blindly and unthinkingly orthodox and loyal to the Party.

Winston's mind shifts back to O'Brien and to the dream in which O'Brien speaks the words, '[w]e shall meet in the place where there is no darkness' (p.27). These words make him feel bonded to O'Brien, despite his uncertainty of their meaning, or even of whether O'Brien is on his side or not. But one thing is certain: Winston feels painfully lonely and cut off from the rest of the world: 'lost in a monstrous world where he himself was the monster' (p.28). He is drawn to O'Brien out of a deep need for connection with another person. For the same reason, he continues to write in his diary. This time his writings express a need to carry on 'the human heritage' (p.30). He writes his testament to the future of humanity. In this humanistic statement, he writes of a future of freedom, of truth, a future in which the uniqueness and individuality of every person are affirmed and safeguarded.

Q Examine the comic elements of this chapter.

Q How are traditional views of children subverted (undermined)?

III (pp.31–9)

Summary: *Winston's dream of his mother. The Golden Country. The Party's falsification of history.*

This chapter opens with Winston's recurring dream of his mother, probably prompted by the scene from the film he has recently seen. Of his mother, long lost to him, he has little conscious memory. It is through dreams, the pathway to the unconscious mind, that he will gain access to memories and thoughts of her, as well as to other aspects of his past. It is the Party's goal to obliterate both the collective and individual memories of people, in order to remove the wider context of their lives and thus increase its control over them. The memory of his mother, like the dream in which it occurs, is highly significant, for it is a memory of unselfish, sacrificial love which comes from 'a conception of loyalty that was private and unalterable' (p.32). Such love, Winston reflects, could not be expressed today, under a regime that forbids the expression of private and familial love.

Julia, at this stage known to Winston (and the reader) as 'the girl with dark hair', also enters the dream. She and Winston are in the place he calls 'the Golden Country', a recurring landscape of his dreams, a place of colour, beauty and freedom. The girl's gesture of tearing off her clothes and flinging them aside 'disdainfully' (p.33) reflects Winston's unconscious sexual desire for her, as well as his unconscious awareness of her desire for him. But the gesture also reflects his unconscious awareness of the girl's contempt for the Party – '[w]ith its grace and carelessness it seemed to annihilate a whole culture, a whole system of thought, as though Big Brother and the Party and the Thought Police could all be swept into oblivion with a single splendid movement of the arm' (p.33). Significantly, Winston wakes with the word 'Shakespeare' on his lips, a name from the forgotten past which symbolises the creative and imaginative greatness of which humans are capable. The Party has now made the expression of this spirit impossible.

At least three things are established in this chapter. The first is that it is only a matter of time before this girl will enter Winston's life in a major way. The second is that Winston is aware that the Party is not merely altering the past, but actually destroying it. The third is that Winston's mind is now beginning to break free of the chains which have kept it captive. The fact that the next chapter begins with the statement that Winston uttered a 'deep, unconscious sigh which not even the telescreen could keep him from uttering' attests to this (p.40).

Q Trace the evolution of Winston's thought throughout this chapter.

Q Explore the motif (recurring image or theme) of dreams, nightmares and memories in this chapter and in the novel as a whole.

IV (pp.40–50)

Summary: *Winston at work in the Ministry of Truth. The rewriting of history.*

Orwell's satirical streak is in play in this chapter, which shows Winston at work in the Ministry of Truth, busily rewriting history. It is ironic that Winston, who seeks to find the truth wherever he can, actually enjoys this work, since he can lose himself in it (p.46). Under the rule of the Party, objective truth no longer exists: real people are 'rubbed out' or 'vaporized', while non-existent people are brought into being – such as the hero Comrade Ogilvy, Winston's invention. We are given a sample of 'Newspeak', the gobbledegook language of Oceania. While activities in this workplace are satirised by Orwell, we can also detect the ever-present sense of menace. The fate of the 'rubbed out' people described here foreshadows Winston's own fate.

Q What skills does Winston bring to his work at the Ministry of Truth?

Q How are the activities of this ministry satirised?

V (pp.51–66)

Summary: *In the canteen at the Ministry of Truth. Syme and the Newspeak dictionary. They discuss the proles. Parsons is introduced. Winston's discontent grows.*

The canteen where this chapter is set is described like an image of hell – 'low-ceilinged canteen, deep under ground' (p.51). Here Winston meets Syme, the Newspeak specialist from the Research Department, a 'venomously orthodox' man who is at work on the new edition of the Newspeak dictionary (p.52). Orwell uses this loathsome man to expound the principles of Newspeak, above all its principal goal of reducing vocabulary in order to reduce its speakers' capacity for thought. All of the great literature of the past will be reduced to Newspeak versions, Syme explains – nothing of the original will be left. The ultimate goal is to prevent people from thinking – the level of orthodoxy (correct, or currently endorsed opinions) which Syme endorses actually means 'not thinking' (p.56).

Parsons, Winston's neighbour at Victory Mansions, is now introduced in person. He praises enthusiastically his children's fanatical zeal in ferreting out 'thoughtcrime' wherever it is to be found. He is, of course, unaware that their zeal will ultimately be turned against him. Apart from his stupidity, his chief distinguishing feature is the repulsiveness of his physical presence, embodied by his prodigious sweating. Indeed, the main emphasis of the latter part of this chapter is the sheer offensiveness of the physical surroundings. Winston 'meditated resentfully on the physical texture of life', wondering if it had always been that way (p.62). The tone of Orwell's description of the surrounding ugliness reflects his anger at the material conditions in which many people are forced to live. Through Winston, Orwell emphasises the importance of beauty as an integral part of a person's quality of life.

Q How is Parsons' stupidity highlighted?

Q Pick out words and phrases which help to depict the ugliness of this environment.

Q Orwell had a deep emotional and intellectual hatred of the death penalty. How is this revealed in this chapter?

VI (pp.66–72)

Summary: *The Party's attitude to sex. Winston's marriage.*

This chapter opens with an entry from Winston's diary, recalling his encounter with a prostitute three years earlier. This memory sets the stage for the main theme of the chapter: the Party's hostility towards sex and Winston's own sexual and emotional life. The Party has made a fulfilling sex life impossible: its stated aim is to remove all pleasure from sex; the only purpose of sexual intercourse is to beget children for the service of the Party. 'Sexual intercourse', we are told, 'was to be looked on as a slightly disgusting minor operation, like having an enema' (p.69). In fact, plans were underway to have all children begotten by artificial insemination ('*artsem*'). The Party intends to redirect the physical and emotional energy expended in sexual activity into the service of the state; the frenzied outpourings of the Two Minutes Hate, for example, are the outcome of repressed sexual feeling.

Winston's estranged wife, Katharine, devotedly followed the Party line on this matter. Their marriage is a bad memory for Winston. Having sex with Katharine was particularly unpleasant: 'embrac[ing] her was like embracing a jointed wooden image' (p.70). Winston cannot suppress his need for a satisfying sex life and this makes him particularly vulnerable to the Party. We are led to sympathise strongly with him in his plight; his hunger is clear when we learn of the awfulness of his encounter with the prostitute.

Q Why does Winston's encounter with the prostitute enter his mind at this stage?

Q What emotions and desires are pressing on Winston?

VII (pp.72–84)

Summary: *Winston's hope for the proles. Jones, Aaronson and Rutherford, and the falsification of history.*

Winston feels that the only hope of overthrowing the regime of the Party lies with the proles, the overwhelming majority of the population, kept powerless because of their ignorance and lack of political consciousness. Winston realises that if they are to rebel against the Party, they need to become conscious, but the problem is that until they rebel, they will never become conscious. Their lack of any broad awareness beyond the everyday realities in which they are mired (stuck) keeps them where the Party wants them.

Winston keeps wondering what life before the Revolution was really like. The children's history textbook, which he borrows from Mrs Parsons, paints a predictable picture of the rule of the wicked capitalists in pre-revolutionary times. The truth is hard to pinpoint, as the Party has done such a thorough job of erasing past history from the public consciousness. Recalling the incident involving Jones, Aaronson and Rutherford, three men who had been executed as traitors, Winston realises that their 'confessions' were lies. He goes on to speculate about the reason for the Party's falsification of history. 'I understand HOW', he writes, 'I do not understand WHY' (p.83). The Party denies the very existence of objective reality. This realisation leads Winston to formulate the axiom (established principle) by which he will stand almost until the end of the story: 'Freedom is the freedom to say that two plus two make four. If that is granted, all else follows' (p.84). There is an inspirational moment near the end of this chapter when we learn that Winston's courage 'seemed suddenly to stiffen of its own accord' (p.84). It bears witness to the heroism of the courageous individual who stands alone against overwhelming odds.

Q What do you think is the significance of the song coming from the telescreen?

Q What aspects of political propaganda does the textbook display about life before the revolution?

VIII (pp.85–107)

Summary: *Winston tries to find out whether life was better before the Revolution. He visits Mr Charrington's junk shop and buys the beautiful paperweight.*

Winston's desire to find out about life before the Revolution leads him to interview an old man, but he is none the wiser for his efforts. The old man is unable to think in any coherent or connected way, so that all Winston can gather are random scraps of information. The world in which they both live lacks a wider context: since the past cannot be recalled, there is nothing against which to compare the present.

Now follows one of the most important parts of the novel, the episode in which Winston visits the junk shop and buys the glass paperweight. It is an object which has survived from an earlier age. It appeals to Winston because, more than anything else, it is a thing of beauty which contrasts starkly with the ugliness of nearly everything else in Oceania. It 'gleamed softly in the lamplight' (p.98) and it seems to represent a world in itself – 'almost a hemisphere' (p.99). Buying this item is a revolutionary act in this society: '[a]nything old, and for that matter anything beautiful, was always vaguely suspect' (p.99). The coral at its centre is an image of the natural world, separate from and uncontaminated by the ugliness of the human world. The paperweight itself, with its softly gleaming beauty, is a yardstick for measuring the corrupted world of Oceania.

Mr Charrington also shows Winston the room above his shop, where Winston and Julia will soon come for their love-making. The room awakens in him 'a sort of nostalgia, a sort of ancestral memory' (p.100), probably a memory of the family home in which he lived as a boy. He is sorely tempted to rent the room, despite the danger. As he walks home, he thinks fearfully of 'the girl', whom he is now sure is spying on him. The ending of the chapter focuses on his sense of inevitability of being arrested by the Thought Police.

Q What are our early impressions of Mr Charrington? How are they contradicted by what we learn about him later?

Q Is a sense of beauty important to quality of life? Why?

Part II (pp.111–234)

I (pp.111–23)

Summary: *Julia and Winston finally meet.*

The danger grows as Julia contrives a way to meet Winston and slips into his hand the piece of paper bearing the words, 'I love you' (p.113). Despite the anxiety these words cause Winston, they strengthen his will to live. When they meet at Victory Square, Julia takes charge of the situation; she has begun to emerge as the stronger, more decisive personality.

Q How is the crucial moment when Winston becomes aware of Julia's love for him highlighted?

Q What range of emotions would Winston be experiencing at this point?

II (pp.123–33)

Summary: *Winston and Julia consummate their relationship in 'the Golden Country'.*

Reading this chapter is a little like seeing a black-and-white film suddenly turn to colour. The setting is like the 'Golden Country', the landscape from Winston's recurring dream. It is interesting to compare this setting, a place of 'dappled light and shade' and 'pools of gold' (p.123) with the monotone setting with which the novel opens. Winston and Julia's love relationship begins in earnest here. It is like a scene from a different story – after all, love relationships are rare in this society. For once, Winston feels unconditionally loved and accepted by another person. His loneliness is assuaged (relieved) and his health, both physical and emotional, soon begins to improve. He is able to get free from his constant mental tension and anxiety as at last he 'stopped thinking and merely felt' (p.130). His dream of Julia flinging aside her clothes in a gesture of contempt for the Party becomes a reality here as he recognises once more 'that same magnificent gesture by which a whole civilisation seemed to be annihilated' (p.131). He recognises that their act of making love is 'a blow struck against the Party ... a political act' (p.133).

Q How is natural beauty represented in this chapter?

Q Track the range of Winston's emotions and thoughts throughout this chapter.

III (pp.133–43)

Summary: *Julia and Winston continue to meet, in the belfry of a bombed-out church. Julia's past history. Winston remembers his wife and the moment when he was tempted to murder her.*

Julia tells Winston about her career in the Youth League and then in the Junior Anti-Sex League. She has played the role of the zealous Party supporter while all the time being fiercely opposed to it. She now works in 'Pornosec', the subsection of the Fiction Department which churns out cheap pornography for the proles. Winston tells Julia about Katharine, his wife, an ultra-orthodox, 'goodthinkful' person – the type Orwell most despised. We learn of the moment during a country hike in which Winston was tempted to push her off the edge of a cliff. It is in keeping with what we know of Winston's appreciation of beauty that he had called his wife to the edge of the cliff in order to observe a beautiful tuft of flowers growing there.

Q What aspects of Julia's personality are revealed in this chapter?

Q Why does the Party encourage the mass production of pornography?

IV (pp.143–54)

Summary: *Winston and Julia meet and make love in the room above Mr Charrington's shop.*

The glass paperweight 'gleamed softly' in the room above Mr Charrington's shop, a symbol of the beautiful world which Winston and Julia are creating for each other. It is a hermetically sealed world (a world untouched by outside influence), like the world inside the paperweight: the beauty is sealed in, the ugliness sealed out. Or so it seems. Mr Charrington appears undisturbed by the activities of Winston and Julia, a fact which on reflection gives cause for concern. Winston is now becoming dependent on his regular sexual contact with Julia even though he considers his actions to be suicidal folly. She seems to have connections everywhere: for example, she arrives at the room in possession of superior quality Inner Party coffee. Winston is horrified to discover that there are rats living in the room; his fear of them is almost pathological.

Q What is the significance of the woman singing underneath the window of the room?

Q Does this chapter contain any elements of a conventional love story? How is it different from a love story?

V (pp.154–63)

Summary: *Syme has vanished, deemed to have 'never existed' (p.154). Preparations for Hate Week are made.*

Syme's disappearance is ominous. In fiercely hot weather, preparations for Hate Week begin. The proles are 'lashed into one of their periodical frenzies of patriotism' (p.156). Winston's health continues to improve. Despite the unsanitary nature of the room in which he and Julia meet, their relationship continues to develop positively. Winston tells Julia of his hopes of fomenting rebellion against the Party. He tells her of the 'strange intimacy' that he feels exists between him and O'Brien, and that he sometimes wishes to just walk in and see him, declaring himself to be an enemy of the Party.

Q Consider what we as readers learn about Mr Charrington here. Are we beginning to become suspicious of him?

Q What is the significance of the story of Jones, Aaronson and Rutherford?

VI (pp.164–7)

Summary: *Winston meets O'Brien at last.*

Winston finally achieves his goal of meeting with O'Brien. O'Brien compliments him on his 'elegant' writing in Newspeak, and recalls discussing this with 'a friend of yours who is certainly an expert'. O'Brien is speaking, of course, of Syme, who is now 'an unperson' (pp.164–5). What has happened to Syme foreshadows Winston's fate, as O'Brien knows, but Winston misreads O'Brien's reference as 'sharing a small act of thoughtcrime' (p.165). Winston knows what that fate will be – 'something that would happen in the Ministry of Love' (p.166) – but he fails to suspect that O'Brien will be involved.

Q Study O'Brien's manner of speech. What impression does this give of him?

Q Is there any evidence that Winston may be unconsciously suspicious of O'Brien?

VII (pp.167–74)

Summary: *Winston's dream about his mother. He discusses the proles with Julia.*

In this chapter, the narrator describes Winston's recurring dream about his mother in the greatest detail so far, poignantly relating Winston's last memory of his mother and his baby sister. Indeed, it is almost unbearably sad, a truly pathetic portrait of a family which is slowly starving to death. The most terrible details concern the baby sister, an infant 'with a face made simian [like a monkey] by thinness' (p.168), clinging to her mother 'with both hands, exactly like a baby monkey' (p.170). It is as if such deep deprivation has pushed this child back to a much earlier, more primitive stage of human development. Perhaps nowhere else in the book do we see – and feel so acutely – Orwell's deep compassion for the sufferings of humans. The family dinner, which culminates in Winston, as a constantly hungry boy, snatching the chocolate away from his sister, is a portrait of the desperate poverty that has always afflicted so many in the world. In the wider context of the novel, the scene reflects Orwell's outrage at the social injustice that makes such poverty a reality.

Desperately sad though it is, the dream contains a positive meaning, one which unconsciously occurs to Winston when he saw the film of the Jewish mother protecting her child. Winston is now fully conscious of that meaning, which is that that '[w]hat mattered were individual relationships, and a completely helpless gesture, an embrace, a tear, a word spoken to a dying man, could have value in itself' (p.172). Winston now reflects back on his action of unthinkingly kicking into the gutter the severed hand lying on the pavement 'as though it had been a cabbage-stalk' (p.172). We can see that Winston's basic humanity is steadily being regenerated. This process of self-understanding seems to have begun with his decision to express his feelings in his diary. He is a man in the process of positive change in the midst of a society that is steadily dehumanising its citizens.

Q What is 'the real point of the story' (p.171)?

Q 'Exactly as his mother had sat on the dingy white-quilted bed, with the child clinging to her, so she had sat in the sunken ship, far underneath him and drowning deeper every minute, but still looking up at him through the darkening water' (p.171). Trace the imagery of drowning and being underwater throughout the novel. What is its significance?

VIII (pp.174–86)

Summary: *Winston and Julia in the Inner Party headquarters. O'Brien arranges for Winston to get a copy of Goldstein's book.*

Finally Winston and Julia are granted entry to the Inner Party headquarters. Life for members of the Inner Party is plainly very much more comfortable than for other citizens. (This strongly echoes the contrast between the pigs, the ruling elite and the other animals in *Animal Farm*: 'All animals are equal but some are more equal than others' (Orwell 1981, p.114).) The telescreen is much less intrusive, the building has luxurious carpeting, there are smells of good food and good tobacco and everything works properly. O'Brien quizzes Winston and Julia about how far they would be prepared to go in their rebellion against the Party. Julia answers, 'No' to the question about her willingness to be permanently separated from Winston. The last paragraph of the chapter is ominous. When O'Brien shakes Winston's hand as he stands up to leave, '[h]is powerful grip crushed the bones of Winston's palm'. Winston looks back, but O'Brien 'seemed already to be in process of putting him out of mind' (p.186). This foreshadows what is soon to come: O'Brien's brutal crushing of Winston, the first stage of the process which will turn him into an 'unperson'.

Q Contrast the description of Inner Party headquarters with other environments described throughout the novel.

Q Imagine what O'Brien might be thinking as he talks with Winston and Julia. Write an internal monologue expressing his thoughts.

IX (pp.186–227)

Summary: *Hate Week. The state's policy is suddenly slammed into reverse. Winston reads Goldstein's book.*

Hate Week has arrived. One of the main purposes of this event is to take the place of sex, to allow the population to release their pent up sexual urges. Orwell suggests this by describing the activities of the week as a 'great orgasm … quivering to its climax' (p.187). At the ministry, Winston struggles against his crushing fatigue, after working more than 90 hours in five days. The cause of this stupendous workload is the Party's announcement that Oceania is, and always has been, at war with Eastasia, not Eurasia. Once again, history is altered at the Party's whim, and with dizzying speed the whole policy of the state is slammed into jolting reverse.

The writing in this section of the chapter has tremendous vitality. This comes from Orwell's keen sense of the ridiculousness of the scenes he describes; his skills as a satirist are fully highlighted here. The vitality comes also the tone of controlled anger at what is being done.

We now reach the interpolated extract from Emmanuel Goldstein's book. Later in the novel we learn that this book was written by O'Brien and other members of the Inner Party. In fact it is a kind of Bible of the Party's philosophy. The vitality with which this chapter opens – indeed, of most of the rest of the novel – sags at this point. Everything included in this section has been expressed with more flair and subtlety elsewhere in the novel. Orwell *tells* his reader what he has already *shown*. His historical analysis and commentary are interesting in themselves, but better suited to a work of non-fiction. Here it sounds didactic (like a lecture) and it impedes the progress of the narrative. It does show, on the other hand, that Julia is uninterested in political philosophy or the world of ideas, lending credence to Winston's jibe that she is 'only a rebel from the waist downwards' (p.163). It also gives us insight into the Party's thinking about the 'two great problems which the Party is concerned to solve' (p.201). The first is 'to discover, against his will, what another human being is thinking' (and thereby to eliminate the possibility of independent thought); the second is 'how to kill several hundred million people in a few seconds without giving warning beforehand' (p.201).

Apart from its informative and analytical content, this section functions to remove the reader for a time from the tension which has been building through the narrative of Winston's trials and of the impending (coming) danger. It lulls both Winston and also perhaps the reader, into a false sense of security. Thereby it heightens the shock when Winston and Julia are arrested by the Thought Police. This is ironic, since what Winston is reading about forecasts his terrible fate: the powerlessness of the individual at the mercy of the all-powerful state.

Q What purpose do you think is served by the inclusion of Goldstein's book?

Q How does language shape our view of the Inner Party writer of Goldstein's book?

X (pp.227–34)

Summary: *Winston and Julia are arrested by the Thought Police.*

Winston feels a surge of optimism as he listens to the woman singing below his window, undaunted by the drudgery of her everyday life. She represents to him a spirit which will one day rise to overthrow oppression and create a new world of sanity. His optimism is quickly and brutally crushed, though, as the

Thought Police surround the room and arrest both him and Julia. Mr Charrington is exposed as an undercover agent of the Thought Police. The glass paperweight is knocked to the floor and smashed, symbolising the smashing of the world which Winston and Julia have created together.

Q The arrest of Winston and Julia is probably the most startling episode in the novel. How is the sense of shock established?

Q How does our view of Mr Charrington change here?

Part III (pp.237–326)

I (pp.237–51)

Summary: *Winston is imprisoned in the Ministry of Love. His interrogation by O'Brien begins.*

Now the horror which has been building through the first two sections of the novel intensifies. Winston is now in a cell in the Ministry of Love: 'the place where there is no darkness'. This expression, we learn, refers to the fact that because there are no windows in the Ministry of Love, the lights are never turned off. It is thus a place where no one can rest peacefully – indeed, it is a place of metaphorical darkness. It is a place of fear, squalor and brutality: the scene in which the prisoner who is ordered to Room 101 resists in terror is deeply shocking (pp.248–9). From this point onwards, Winston embodies the political prisoner of our age – perhaps of all ages – as the narrative is concentrated intensely on his interrogation and torture by O'Brien. No one seems safe from the Thought Police – Ampleforth the poet is there, apparently merely because he could not find an appropriate rhyming word other than 'God'. Even Parsons, the model of grovelling obedience, is there, turned in by his children after cursing Big Brother in his sleep. And there is a vulgar but amiable woman named Smith: Winston wonders if she could be his long lost mother.

Q What do you make of the incident involving the woman named Smith?

Q Do you feel any sympathy for Parsons?

II (pp.251–73)

Summary: *Winston is tortured and 'confesses' everything. O'Brien shows Winston the photographs of Jones, Aaronson and Rutherford and tells him that these people never existed.*

The intensity of Winston's ordeal intensifies. O'Brien tells Winston that he is 'mentally deranged' (p.258) and that he aims to 'make [Winston] sane' (p.265). He describes Winston as 'a lunatic, a minority of one' (p.261). He also states that reality 'exists in the human mind, and nowhere else' (p.261), thus denying the validity of external, objective reality. Reality and truth are what the Party says they are. Despite O'Brien's cruelty, Winston still feels dependent on him. In spite of everything, O'Brien is 'a person who could be talked to' (p.264).

O'Brien conducts his 'how many fingers am I holding up?' test. He explains to Winston that he is torturing him because 'we make the brain perfect before we blow it out' (p.267). All this is chilling, but even here Orwell allows us a moment of black comic relief. 'Your mind appeals to me', O'Brien tells Winston. 'It resembles my own except that you happen to be insane' (p.271).

Q How does this chapter clarify the idea of doublethink?

Q How does the narrator's language persuade us of the horror of Winston's ordeal?

III (pp.273–87)

Summary: *O'Brien reveals the Party's true motive – power for its own sake.*

O'Brien explains to Winston that the Party authorities 'are not interested in the good of others'; on the contrary, they are interested 'solely in power' (p.275). In acknowledging this, he tells Winston, they have gone even beyond the German Nazis and the Russian Communists, who 'never had the courage to recognise their own motives' (p.276). (The German Nazis and the Russian Communists represent the most extreme and brutal forms of government of the twentieth century.) Here Orwell is expressing one of the most important insights of the novel: that many rulers indeed do come to seek and exercise power for its own sake. He shows us, too, the often intimate connection between power and sadism. Human beings assert their power over others by making them suffer, Winston realises.

Despite the torture he is undergoing, Winston is still able to tell O'Brien that he believes that 'the spirit of Man' will prevail over tyranny. And, also despite the torture, Winston still feels a 'peculiar reverence' for his torturer (p.286).

Q What does O'Brien mean when he says that '[t]he heretic, the enemy of society, will always be there, so that he can be defeated and humiliated over again' (p.270)?

Q What makes us sympathise with Winston in the dialogue between Winston and O'Brien?

IV (pp.287–95)

Summary: *Winston works at 're-educating' himself.*

Winston begins to get much stronger physically. For a time, his torture is stopped and his body given a chance to recover. He has capitulated to O'Brien and, as a result, begins to work at the task of 're-educating' himself (p.289). He writes doublethink propositions of the Party, such as 'FREEDOM IS SLAVERY', the nonsensical 'TWO AND TWO MAKE FIVE' and finally 'GOD IS POWER', a proposition affirming the Party's emphasis on power rather than love. From this point in the novel, Winston starts to accept the Party's teachings. The writing has a bitterly ironic force, as can be seen in Winston's realisation that '[s]tupidity was as necessary as intelligence, and as difficult to attain' (p.292).

Despite his efforts at 're-education', Winston falters when he cries out 'Julia, my love' in his sleep (p.293). He has a powerful sense of her presence, which is perhaps telepathic: he has an intuition that she is 'still alive and needed his help' (p.293). As a result of this incident, he is questioned by O'Brien again and he admits that he still hates Big Brother (p.295). O'Brien decides that Winston is now ready to be sent to Room 101, the most dreaded room in the Ministry of Love.

Q What does the term 're-education' show about how totalitarian governments view 'education'?

Q In writing 'GOD IS POWER' (p.290), Winston alters the well-known saying, 'God is love'. In what ways does the novel show us the differences between power and love?

V (pp.295–300)

Summary: *Winston is tortured in Room 101 and betrays Julia.*

In this, one of the most horrific episodes in the novel, Winston is taken to Room 101, the torture centre most deeply dreaded by all prisoners. Confronted by the threat of his greatest fear, feral rats, his resistance completely crumbles as he betrays Julia with the words, 'Do it to Julia!' (p.300). This represents the Party's final victory over Winston: he has been forced to subordinate his basic humanity and individuality to the state. Everyone has a breaking point: O'Brien knows this and finds Winston's.

Q Examine the ways in which Orwell illustrates O'Brien's sadism.

Q Why does O'Brien want Winston and Julia to betray each other?

VI (pp.300–11)

Summary: *Winston's final days. He 'loves Big Brother'.*

A mere shell of a man, his spirit completely broken, Winston spends what we can imagine will be his final days sitting alone in the Chestnut Tree Café. In a zombie-like state, he writes the equation 2 + 2 = 5 on the tablecloth. He sees Julia again, but all the spark of their old relationship is gone. Each admits to betraying the other. He recalls another memory from his childhood, this time a happy episode in which he, his mother and his sister played a game of Snakes and Ladders. The effect of the inclusion of this memory at this point is desperately sad. Orwell is showing us that this is where sanity really lies, in the happy and intimate connections between people who love each other. This underscores the terrible irony of the final sentence of the novel: 'He loved Big Brother' (p.311). We come to the end of this chapter, and to the end of the novel as a whole, with the wrung out feeling that one is left with at the end of a Greek tragedy. The tone of the writing supports this sense of exhaustion, too.

Q Comment on how the idea of 'victory' is explored in this chapter.

Q What is your response to the end of the novel?

CHARACTERS & RELATIONSHIPS

Winston Smith

Key quotes

'He felt as though he were wandering in the forests of the sea bottom, lost in a monstrous world where he himself was the monster. He was alone.' (p.28)

'... the sense of his own inferiority was heavy upon him.' (p.124)

'He was a lonely ghost uttering a truth that nobody would ever hear.' (p.30)

Winston as 'the last man'

Orwell contemplated entitling his novel *The Last Man*, a concept which emerges during an exchange late in the novel between Winston and O'Brien. After Winston tells his persecutor that 'the spirit of Man' will eventually defeat the Party, O'Brien replies, 'If you are a man, Winston, you are the last man' (p.282). 'The spirit of Man', for Winston, is the humanistic spirit which seeks to affirm and defend the dignity of humanity, and to preserve and 'carry on the human heritage', as the narrator puts it earlier in the novel (p.30). If, to O'Brien, Winston is 'the last man', then he is the last human to have retained his essential humanity in the midst of a race of dehumanised people. By the end of the narrative, of course, we see him utterly broken by the Party, emptied of his best humanity and waiting passively for his death. But it seems to me that this does not negate the value of what he has been or of what he has come to represent.

Winston as hero?

At first, Winston seems an unlikely hero, especially if we have in mind the notion of the hero as outwardly impressive, commanding and physically attractive. Although only 39, Winston is falling apart physically. He drinks gin all day long to take the edge off a consciousness which is always painful. He has little sense of his value as a human being – hardly surprising, since nothing ever seems to have happened to him to affirm that value. When Julia falls in love with him, for example, he asks her how she could possibly be interested in him.

And yet, for most of the novel he lives with a stubborn, stoic spirit, just putting one foot in front of the other and going on with his life. Sometimes, the bravest act can simply be to get up in the morning and keep going, and so it is for a man like Winston, who carries the burden of his everyday life like a crushing weight. He is a man beaten down by the oppression that surrounds him, yet he still retains the spirit to resist. For most of the story, he keeps alive a spirit of hope and of optimism. Even though he senses deep within that his fate is sealed from the moment he opens his diary and begins to write down his subversive ideas, he keeps writing, affirming his individuality and dignity as a human being.

At least a part of the impulse that drives him to keep a diary arises from his deep intellectual curiosity. He is constantly seeking to *understand* why things are as they are. This desire underpins his dual statement about the Party's deliberate falsification of history: 'I understand HOW: I do not understand WHY' (p.83). His hunger to understand the meaning of his life leads him on a quest to uncover his own past life and that of his society. We feel his mind working, through dream and through memory to bring these to light.

One could use the word hunger to describe Winston's intellectual curiosity; indeed, that word applies to him in a number of different ways. One of his key childhood memories is of constant physical hunger. As an adult, he is a deeply lonely man with a hunger for connections with others. When he begins his relationship with Julia, we sense just how lonely and isolated he has been, how deprived of any kind of intimacy. How deep that unfulfilled need has been is apparent from the marked improvement in his physical and emotional well-being after he forms that relationship. And the way he gravitates towards O'Brien can largely be explained by his need to talk to someone about what is in his mind, a need so pressing that it blinds him to the danger that O'Brien poses. He so much *wants* this man to be a soul mate that he manages to convince himself that he really is.

Winston also hungers for beauty. He feels a visceral revulsion against the surrounding ugliness; 'he meditated resentfully on the physical texture of life' (p.62). This coarse 'physical texture' rubs against him all the more abrasively as he has a deep sense of the beautiful. He gets a sensual pleasure from feeling the smooth, creamy paper of the antique notebook in which he writes; he is captivated by the beauty of the glass paperweight as it shines softly. The coral inside it appeals to him because it illustrates the beauty of the natural world, which human beings can never completely besmirch. Significantly, his unconscious mind conjures up the beautiful place which he calls 'the Golden Country'. There, with Julia, he experiences episodes of liberation and delight.

If we look beyond the last image we have of Winston in the novel, that of a ruined shell of a man – and he can hardly be blamed for this fate – we can see many positive, indeed even heroic, images of him. We can see him, too, as a person who is capable of growth. His diary entries show a process of growing understanding and awareness of himself and of his world. The unshaped recollections of the previous night's movie (pp.10–11) give way to the strong, optimistic testament of hope for a future 'when thought is free, when men are different from one another and do not live alone' (p.30). Later, he reflects with some shock on his action of unthinkingly kicking the severed hand into the gutter, a sign that his blunted humanity is returning. And his relationship with Julia shows that he is capable of giving himself to another person on every level.

Julia and her relationship with Winston

Key quotes

'She had immediately taken charge of the situation, just as she had done in the canteen.' (p.121)
'Almost as swiftly as he had imagined it, she had torn her clothes off, and when she flung them aside it was with that same magnificent gesture by which a whole civilisation seemed to be annihilated.' (p.131)
'With Julia, everything came back to her own sexuality. As soon as this was touched upon in any way she was capable of great acuteness.' (p.139)
'In some ways she was far more acute than Winston, and far less susceptible to Party propaganda.' (p.160)

The focus of Winston's life is in his mind; the focus of Julia's life is in her body. In vital respects, her personality complements Winston's. He is highly cerebral; she is highly sexual and sensual. It is ironic that many of her 26 years have been spent in the Youth League and then the Junior Anti-Sex League, organisations which both slavishly follow the Party's fundamental opposition to sex and sexuality. Most likely she has made herself prominent in these organisations in order to mask her true feelings and inclinations.

Her vitality, both of body and of spirit, is perhaps her most attractive quality. Almost as soon as Winston begins his relationship with her, she begins to lift his spirits. His physical and emotional health improves greatly. Her commitment to life makes her a life-giving person. Winston's mournful reflection that 'so long as human beings stay human, death and life are the same thing', brings the rebuke: 'Oh, rubbish! Which would you sooner sleep with, me or a skeleton?' (p.142). The question reveals a strong sense of her own worth which the rule of the Party has obviously failed to crush.

That quality is immediately evident from the way in which she initiates contact with Winston and then plays the leading role in the formation of their relationship. During their initial meeting in Victory Square, she sets up their next meeting with 'a sort of military precision that astonished him' (p.121). Her strong personality is also on display when she flings off her clothes 'with that same magnificent gesture by which a whole civilisation seemed to be annihilated' (p.131). She has a contempt for authority which makes her 'far less susceptible to Party propaganda' than Winston (p.160). Winston hates the Party and everything it represents, yet he is still impressed by O'Brien's powerful air of authority, to an extent that Julia never would be.

Julia has an enormously positive influence on Winston's life, but it is hard to imagine that their relationship would have been entirely satisfying to either if circumstances had allowed it to continue. While Julia lacks intellectual curiosity, Winston has it in abundance. The point is made when Julia drifts off to sleep while Winston reads to her from Goldstein's book. She is utterly bored by something he finds absorbing. Yet the two share a strong mutual respect and love: Julia's simple and direct statement to Winston 'I love you' is one he is fully able to reciprocate.

O'Brien

Key quotes

'His heavy face ... looked both formidable and intelligent.' (pp.175–6)
'He had the feeling that O'Brien was his protector ...' (p.263)
'The old feeling, that at bottom it did not matter whether O'Brien was a friend or an enemy, had come back. O'Brien was a person who could be talked to.' (p.264)
'We are not interested in the good of others, we are interested solely in power.' (p.275)
'The peculiar reverence for O'Brien, which nothing seemed able to destroy, flooded Winston's heart again.' (p.286)

O'Brien, Winston's nemesis (a person or force that inflicts punishment or revenge), represents evil hidden under a civilised veneer. Winston is deeply drawn to him by his face when he first sees him, and persuades himself that he is a man whom he can talk to, someone who will relieve his sense of lonely isolation in the world. Winston wants him to be a kind of father-figure, or protector to him, and he persuades himself that that is what he is. Although O'Brien's face is often described as 'ugly', 'brutal' and 'formidable', it is also described as 'humorous', 'intelligent' and even 'in some indefinable way, curiously civilised' (p.12). From the early stages of the narrative he is described with these contradictory adjectives, as if Orwell is deliberately setting out to make him a figure of mystery.

The mystery remains through the scenes in Part II of the novel in which he welcomes Winston and Julia into the Inner Party headquarters and leads them to believe that he is their partner in thoughtcrime. It is not until the final section of the novel, when we see him carrying out his job in the Ministry of Love, that his mask is completely stripped away and we see his true nature. His face may convey an impression of complexity, but underneath that he is little more than a brute. What Winston reads as reassuring strength is cold, dispassionate cruelty. The fanatical gleam can be seen in his eyes as he reveals his true identity as a man who has channelled all his energies into the pursuit and enjoyment of power for its own sake. 'The object of power is power' (p.276), he tells Winston, and in the act of exercising his own power there seems to be nothing of which he is incapable. He displays a degree of sadism that allows him to commit any torture while never batting an eyelid.

This makes him an interesting figure, since he so far exceeds the boundaries of civilised behaviour. He represents the evildoer who knows exactly what he is doing and is quite comfortable with it. He is seems like the Nazi functionaries who committed mass murder by day at Auschwitz, the notorious Nazi concentration camp in Poland where millions of Jews were murdered. They returned home to their families at night apparently undisturbed, like men returning home from a normal day at work. He tortures Winston and spouts the transparent nonsense of the Party he serves as if what he is doing is completely natural. There is a grotesque disjunction between his controlled and apparently reasonable manner and his conduct.

And so it is that what Winston hoped would be a relationship between kindred spirits, if not equals, becomes a relationship between the persecutor and the persecuted. In their encounter in the Ministry of Love, O'Brien reduces Winston to the status of an object to be blasted out of the way: 'We shall turn you into gas and pour you into the stratosphere', he claims (p.266).

Big Brother

Key quotes

'... the poster with the enormous face gazed from the wall. It was one of those pictures which are so contrived that the eyes follow you about when you move. BIG BROTHER IS WATCHING YOU, the caption beneath it ran.' (p.3)
'Big Brother is the embodiment of the Party.' (p.272)
'The hypnotic eyes gazed into his own. It was as though some huge force were pressing down upon you – something that penetrated inside your skull, battering against your brain, frightening you out of your beliefs, persuading you, almost, to deny the evidence of your senses.' (p.83)

Although Big Brother is not a flesh-and-blood character, his name has become so familiar since the publication of this novel that he must be discussed here. His significance lies in what he represents: the unchecked power of the state over the individual. His name has come to stand for the menace of totalitarian government. He is a concept, an idea, the embodiment of the invincibility of the Party. He represents a key aspect of the Party's myth-making: the idea that all citizens can be placed under surveillance at all times. He is as much a myth as the Old Testament idea of God as a harsh, unforgiving and terrifying figure who lives above the world in the heavens. The Party substitutes Big Brother for that God. Like God, he can be everywhere at the same time, and, of course, immortal. The Party has clearly set him up as a quasi-religious figure of devotion for the people.

His name is a travesty of the traditional idea of a big brother as a loving and protective member of a family. This is ironic in a state that has systematically destroyed the concept of family bonds. Ironically, his name is also a travesty of the ideal of human brotherhood promoted by communist philosophy.

Parsons and Syme – representative types

Key quotes

'In an intellectual way, Syme was venomously orthodox. He would talk with a disagreeable gloating satisfaction of helicopter raids on enemy villages, the trials and confessions of thought-criminals, the executions in the cellars of the Ministry of Love.' (p.52)

'One of these days, thought Winston with sudden deep conviction, Syme will be vaporized. He is too intelligent. He sees too clearly and speaks too plainly.' (p.56)

'[Parsons] was a fattish but active man of paralysing stupidity, a mass of imbecile enthusiasms – one of those completely unquestioning, devoted drudges on whom, more even than on the Thought Police, the stability of the Party depended.' (p.24)

Syme and Parsons, though vastly different in terms of personality and intellectual capacity – as the above quotations show – are linked because they each represent the deep orthodoxy and conformity that Orwell clearly despises. (Winston's estranged wife Katharine, the 'goodthinkful' supporter of the Party, also represents this characteristic.) Orwell also uses Syme, the expert in Newspeak, to outline the essential principles of that language. Syme is the worst kind of zealot (fanatic) – not only taking pleasure in the destruction of words ('a beautiful thing') (p.54), but also exhibiting a sadistic relish at the cruelties which the Party inflicts on its enemies. He illustrates the truth that a high level of intelligence is no guarantee of humane thought or behaviour. It is difficult to feel much distress at the thought of Syme's eventual vaporisation – he merely becomes the victim of the kind of cruelty, which he has enjoyed seeing directed against others.

The depiction of Parsons is amusing, despite – or perhaps because of – the fact that he is so repulsive. He is a model of sycophantic obedience to Big Brother, who is so stupid –like an overgrown boy scout – and also so physically unpleasant, with his extreme sweating. He ends up as a pathetic victim of his hero, Big Brother, still clinging to his Party loyalty, wracked with remorse over his thoughtcrime. His fate is not surprising considering that his children are such zealous pupils of the Party that they are prepared to turn in any 'thought-criminal', even if he happens to be their father.

THEMES, IDEAS & VALUES

Totalitarianism and the suffering it causes

Key quote

> 'If you want a picture of the future, imagine a boot stamping on a human face – for ever.' (p.280)

O'Brien's chilling vision of the future – 'a boot stamping on a human face' – is the defining image of life under the rule of the Party and Big Brother. A recurring motif throughout the novel is the human face reflecting and embodying everything which makes us unique and individual. Orwell's biographer, Michael Shelden, remarks that 'throughout Orwell's work, he is constantly stressing the importance of the human face' (1991, p.314). Winston is drawn to O'Brien because of what he sees – or imagines he sees – in his face. Julia is attracted to Winston because of 'something in your face' (p.128). Parsons' face reflects his stupidity. The terrifying face of Big Brother represents the face of the Party's evil, an evil which sets out to crush the humanity of its subjects. In the scene in the Ministry of Truth in which the unnamed prisoner is being dragged off to Room 101, he 'looked frantically round at the other prisoners', his eyes settling on 'the smashed face of [a] chinless man' (p.249). And it is with a bitterly ironic tone that the novel ends with the image of Winston 'gazing' up lovingly at the face of Big Brother: the face which symbolises the boot in his own face (p.311).

The face of Big Brother represents the exercise of power for its own sake. One of the most important insights of this novel is that a disturbing link exists between sadism and the lust for power. As Winston realises, one man can assert his power over another '[b]y making him suffer' (p.279). O'Brien explains the sadistic mentality of the torturer, telling Winston that 'power is in inflicting pain and humiliation' and also 'in tearing human minds to pieces and putting them together again in new shapes of your own choosing' (p.279). 'Progress', for O'Brien, is 'progress towards more pain' (p.279).

Orwell's depiction of the results of unregulated power has proved to be remarkably accurate. Many regimes today do little more than inflict misery on their people, as a glance at any Amnesty International newsletter demonstrates. It is easy for us, living in a country with a democratic system of government with checks and balances, to forget about those governments which are accountable to no one and do not tolerate dissent.

Q Which freedoms that we take for granted in Australia are taken from the people of Oceania?

Q In the novel, the use of power is generally presented in a very negative light. Is it ever presented in a more positive light?

The manipulation of language

One of the principal ways in which the Party maintains and extends its control over its subjects, is through the conscious manipulation and perversion of language. Its chief instrument in doing this is, of course, Newspeak, its pared-to-the-bone, staccato corruption of English. Like everything else that bears the Party's stamp, it is ugly – sometimes when spoken it sounds like the quacking of a duck. As the official language of Oceania, Newspeak is specifically designed to help prevent thoughtcrime, the holding of unorthodox ideas and thoughts, 'the essential crime that contained all others in itself' (p.21). The language's vocabulary is steadily narrowed and restricted. Any words containing ambiguity or subtlety of meaning are eliminated. The purpose of this vocabulary reduction is to limit the range of thought and thereby the possibility of expressing irregular ideas.

The words needed to express such ideas simply disappear. And so a document such as the American Declaration of Independence, a model for a liberal democracy to follow, can be dismissed with the single word 'crimethink' (p.325).

Language as slogan and doublethink

In the world of Oceania, language is twisted and manipulated by being reduced to slogans, which are usually statements of doublethink – the capacity to argue that black is white, that the patently illogical makes sense. Hence we see contradictory words placed side by side, such as 'WAR IS PEACE', 'FREEDOM IS SLAVERY' and 'IGNORANCE IS STRENGTH'. The same grotesque incongruity of such slogans is reminiscent of the slogan placed above the gate to the Nazi concentration camp Auschwitz translated as 'Work makes free'. In Oceania, language is always misleading. The expression 'the place where there is no darkness', for example, suggests an idyllic place of light, until we discover that it refers to the Ministry of Love, and that the only reason there is no darkness there, is that the lights are never switched off.

Q How does Orwell's own style of writing differ from Newspeak?

The falsification of history

Key quotes

'Nothing exists except an endless present in which the Party is always right.' (p.162)
'All history was a palimpsest, scraped clean and re-inscribed exactly as often as was necessary.' (p.42)

No analysis of *Nineteen Eighty-Four* would be complete without a discussion of the Party's deliberate policy of falsifying history – a common feature of totalitarian regimes. The 'memory hole', that ingenious device by which inconvenient facts can be annulled, is perhaps the chief symbol of this policy. The facts of history are what the Party says they are; that is why Orwell describes history as 'a palimpsest' – that is, a document which is erased so that something else can be written over the top of it. The old man whom Winston questions about earlier times is presumably representative of most of the citizens of Oceania. Their minds have been so manipulated by the constant and confusing barrage of Party propaganda that they are no longer able to recall clearly anything of substance from the past. We might also suspect that Victory Gin has been supplied to the population in such liberal quantities because alcohol abuse is known to impair the human capacity for memory.

The destruction of memory and the falsification of history are terrible because they falsify the whole meaning of human experience. The past – whether individual or collective – is a collection of memories, and memories tell the story of our lives. To a large degree, we are what we remember. The rulers of Oceania, of course, understand this and that is why they seek to obliterate the memory of the past. If our memories are destroyed, then so too are our individual and collective identities. This is why Winston constantly struggles to resurrect both his own personal history and the history of Oceania. He understands the need for one's life to have a wider context than the 'endless present'. This is why he seeks to preserve 'the human heritage', because the legacy of the past enables us to understand the present.

Q Explore Winston's memories as they are described throughout the novel. Is there a pattern to them? Do they contain any recurring themes?

Q What does the novel show us about the nature of memory?

The loneliness of the dissenter

Key quotes

'For a second, two seconds, they had exchanged an equivocal glance, and that was the end of the story. But even that was a memorable event in the locked loneliness in which one had to live.' (p.20)

'He felt as though he were wandering in the forests of the sea bottom, lost in a monstrous world in which he was the monster.' (p.28)

'If you are a man, Winston, you are the last man.' (p.282)

Winston's decision to stand alone in dissent against the rule of Big Brother, to make himself 'a minority of one' exacerbates the loneliness which is a dominant feature of his life. He gets no pleasure from the endless communal activities organised by the Party which are designed to destroy individual life. These activities, indeed, are a parody of genuine connection with others; all they do is to strengthen the Party's stranglehold over the individual. In a sense, Winston is never really alone, since the telescreens and Thought Police are constantly watching him. But in truth he is terribly alone, since he is forced to retreat deeply into himself in an effort to try to protect himself from this constant violation of privacy.

Winston hungers for genuine connection with other people. This makes him vulnerable to O'Brien's deceit, but it also enables him to form a life-giving love relationship with Julia. Throughout the novel, Orwell's motif of the human face and the expressions it shows reflects that deep, universal need of humans to connect with each other.

Q *Nineteen Eighty-Four* shows that, ultimately, we are all alone. Do you agree?

Q Why does Winston continue to oppose the Party even when he knows how dangerous this is?

Values

What makes life worth living?

In *Nineteen Eighty-Four*, George Orwell implicitly addresses the question: what makes life worth living? Even in the dark world of the novel, a world in which there appears to be so little that is praiseworthy, Orwell shows us positive values and qualities, such as the courage and spirit of Winston and Julia. But the main way in which he shows us what he endorses is by showing us what he opposes. After all, for every 'no', there is a corresponding 'yes'. One way of reading the novel is to see the way the author sets up a series of oppositions between opposing values, showing the tensions between them.

The great Viennese psychoanalyst, Sigmund Freud, formulated what he saw as a central opposition within the human mind between a life force (Eros) and a death force (Thanatos). (These two terms were not intended to define 'life' and 'death' as merely biological states, rather these words convey particular attitudes. That is, the life force enhances life and leads to growth, whereas the death force diminishes life and leads to stagnation.) In *Nineteen Eighty-Four*, a tension between life and death forces is revealed within society. All of the key oppositions in the novel are related to that central tension. Generally speaking, it is the Party and those who follow it blindly who represent the death force; those who stand up for freedom of thought and expression represent the life force. We can assume that the values of characters presented sympathetically, such as Winston, are generally the values endorsed by the author. Conversely, the values of characters presented unsympathetically are probably values rejected by the author.

Q Can you see any positive elements in the view of life presented in the novel?

Q What keeps Winston going through the trials he faces?

Freedom versus repression

The Party has locked its citizens into the straitjacket of a single ideology –'Ingsoc' – an ideology according to which freedom of thought is the most serious crime. The goal of the mass rallies and 'spontaneous demonstrations' organised by the Party is complete uniformity of thought – the mind control of the population. Indeed, one of the unrealised goals of the Party is to discover a way of knowing what people are thinking, of invading even the private mind-space of individuals. Winston's opposition to the Party philosophy, recorded in one of his earliest diary entries, is a humanistic testament to freedom of thought. Winston imagines 'a time when thought is free, when men are different from each other and do not live alone – ... a time when truth exists and what is done cannot be undone' (p.30).

Q Does the novel suggest that without freedom, life is not worth living?

Q Examine how the Party sets out to stifle freedom of thought and expression.

Vitality versus stagnation

The dominant impression of the world of Big Brother is of a world stripped of all vitality and spirit. Everyone – except members of the Inner Party, of course – seems to be in terrible physical condition, not least Winston, whose physical ailments are detailed at a very early stage of the narrative. Living in this society blunts the senses. It is not surprising, then, that Winston numbers himself among 'the dead'. But set against these images of stagnation, is the image of Julia's vitality of mind, body and spirit. She infuses some of that vitality into Winston. She has an optimism which attracts life; she cuts through Winston's pessimism, telling him to 'stop talking about dying' (p.143).

Q What does Winston mean when he says, 'We are the dead' (p.230)?

Q What qualities help to lift a person out of a state of deadness in *Nineteen Eighty-Four*?

Cruelty versus humanity

The rule of the Party has brutalised the people. We observe this from the novel's first chapter, in which Winston's diary reveals the film audience's delighted response to the violent scene that is unfolding on the screen. A little later, we see the savagery which is being bred into children, through the viciousness of the Parsons children. And then, we see Syme approvingly relating the details of the latest public executions. All of this is the outgrowth of the Party's policy of constantly fomenting hate and fear of 'enemies', whether internal or external.

Winston Smith is a man capable of standing aside from that brutality, in fact, of growing beyond it. We see this later when he recognises his own callousness in instinctive kicking aside the severed hand lying on the pavement. In the protective gesture of the Jewish mother sheltering her child, and also in the similar gesture of his own mother, he recognises a basic humanity without which life will always be degraded.

Q Trace Winston's growth in moral awareness throughout the story.

Q What specific aspects of the Party's rule exemplify its brutality?

Sanity versus madness

O'Brien judges Winston to be insane because he has chosen to be 'a minority of one' (p.261). The reality is that what O'Brien, on behalf of the Party, represents is insane: the idea implied is that no external, objective reality exists, that '[n]othing exists except through human consciousness' (p.278). Orwell shows us that sanity lies in the strength of mind to defend what we know to be true. In the fanaticism of O'Brien lies madness; in the open-minded intellectual curiosity of Winston lies sanity.

Q O'Brien appears to be sane, yet much of what he says is quite mad. How would you explain this apparent contradiction?

Q Why do you think the Party judges those who oppose it to be insane?

Beauty versus ugliness

Almost everything in Oceania is ugly; it is a world in which 'there seemed to be no colour in anything' (p.4). Winston feels visceral revulsion against the 'physical texture' (p.62) of the world. This writing has a tone of barely suppressed anger. But *Nineteen Eighty-Four* also shows us those things of beauty that help to counteract the surrounding ugliness. Like jewels hidden on a rubbish heap, we are shown the beautiful paperweight; the 'smooth, creamy' (p.8) texture of the paper in Winston's diary; the liberating openness and colour of the Golden Country; even the unusual kind of beauty which Winston sees in the woman singing beneath his window. *Nineteen Eighty-Four* shows us that beauty enhances our quality of life, and conversely, that ugliness impairs it.

Q How does the novel represent the natural world?

Q Do you think that the novel suggests that there is a connection between environmental ugliness and ugliness of mind?

DIFFERENT INTERPRETATIONS

'Everyone reads a different book', goes the saying. There is never any one entirely 'correct' interpretation of a work of literature. That is not to say that some interpretations are not more convincing than others, or that any interpretation is valid because 'it's my opinion' (as students sometimes like to say). What matters is that your reading of a text can be validated by means of supporting evidence from it. In the final analysis, the words on the page are what matters. They are always there, supporting or refuting our interpretation. Here are two different, but possible, readings of *Nineteen Eighty-Four*.

1 In *Nineteen Eighty-Four,* Orwell presents an overwhelmingly bleak view of humanity.

It is possible to see *Nineteen Eighty-Four* as a deeply pessimistic work which offers little or no hope for the future of humanity. There is an unrelenting mood of darkness from the beginning to the end. The world of Oceania is grey and oppressive; all the citizens are intimidated by the Party and by the ubiquitous face of Big Brother which looks down menacingly upon them. Freedom of thought is impossible because of the prevalence of the Thought Police, who are constantly on the lookout for evidence of thoughtcrime. In this society, people have been cut off from the wider context of their lives, both individual and collective. This is because the Party controls the past by manipulating the facts. The result is that 'nothing exists except an endless present in which the Party is always right' (p.162).

Furthermore, there is no character in the story who we can unreservedly admire. Winston Smith starts out determined to seek the truth about life prior to the Revolution, and to stand up in opposition to the tyranny of Party rule. However, he submits to

O'Brien under torture, betrays Julia, and then tries to 're-educate himself' so that he can accept the teachings of the Party. He finally surrenders his integrity of mind by reaching the conclusion that 'he loved Big Brother' (p.311). Julia, like Winston, has independence of mind and a spirited contempt for the Party. Yet she, too, betrays the one she loves under torture. It can also be argued that her hatred of the Party springs from a purely personal anger at the way its policies towards sex have prevented her from expressing her strong sexual needs. Unlike Winston, she has little interest, for example, in improving life for the wider society so that a better future may be created for all. Other characters, such as Parsons and Syme, are revoltingly sycophantic towards Big Brother and the rulers of the Party; they constantly try to outdo others in their loyalty towards this vile regime.

But by the far the darkest part of the novel is Part III. The pessimism of the ending is the last – and strongest – impression with which the reader is left. There is a tone of bitter irony and even despair in the final words of the novel, which tell us that 'Winston had won the victory over himself', since finally '[h]e loved Big Brother' (p.311). This is a powerful image of the crushing of the individual by the might of the state. The earlier hope that Winston might finally prevail against Big Brother is totally lost. We are left deflated by this realisation. There is much else, too, in the last section of the novel, which testifies to the deep cruelty and sadism of which humans are capable when they have unchecked power. The descriptions of the torture of prisoners, including of course, Winston, are deeply shocking. O'Brien turns Winston into an object to be merely 'turned into gas and poured into the stratosphere' (p.266). The boot has stamped all over the human face and crushed it to a pulp. *Nineteen Eighty-Four* is an elegy for the suffering of humanity at the hands of tyrants – it offers an utterly bleak view of humanity.

2 *Nineteen Eighty-Four* tells the story of a courageous struggle for truth and freedom against overwhelming odds, and we can find a measure of inspiration in this.

It is very easy to be overcome by a sense of deep pessimism over the future of humanity when reading *Nineteen Eighty-Four*. After all, the storyline is very bleak, describing as it does the ultimate defeat of the individual at the hands of an apparently all-powerful state. We cannot ignore the bitter irony of the last words of the novel which describe Winston Smith, broken and beaten, as having at last 'won the victory over himself' now that he 'loved Big Brother' (p.311). We are entitled to feel cheated of our hope that the novel's hero might have won the victory over the Party and its embodiment, Big Brother. We feel wrung out after the experience of reading about the tortures that Winston has undergone at the hands of O'Brien in the interrogation and torture centre, so inappropriately named 'the Ministry of Love'.

Yet I argue that there is more to the novel than this, we can find inspiration in it. For even though Winston fails to avoid his final, terrible fate, his personal struggle has value in itself, despite its ultimate failure. Though he is thwarted at every turn, deceived horribly by O'Brien, a man in whom he had placed his trust, he can be seen to be following the pathway of other courageous dissidents, whose rebellion has helped to change life for the better. In a world of doublespeak, lies and falsifications, Winston is a seeker of truth. He strives to find out the truth not only about his own past, but also about the collective past of his society. He embodies a spirit of intellectual curiosity which has always enhanced the quality of human life. His personal testament is formulated in his diary: he envisages 'a time when thought is free, when men are different from each other and do not live alone' (p.30), a time 'when truth exists and what is done cannot be undone' (p.30). While we have to admit that such a vision of the future is unlikely to become a reality in the world of Big Brother, we should also keep in mind the value of those ideals which Orwell, through his central character, has placed before us. Yes, it is true that tyranny causes enormous misery for those who live under its heel, but it can never entirely crush the hunger for a better future and the courage to strive for it.

There is something inspiring, too, in the love relationship which Winston and Julia manage to form. Their courage in defying the Party's prohibitions is admirable. Julia herself is a life-giving person. She infuses some of her vitality into Winston. The brutal way in which their relationship is terminated is certainly saddening, but we can reflect that it was better for their relationship to have existed, even if only briefly, than for it not to have existed at all.

I find this interpretation of the novel more appealing than the one outlined above. In support of this Christopher Booker argues that Orwell unknowingly predicted the later collapse of communist totalitarianism, as seen in such events as the Solidarity movement in Poland, the demolition of the Berlin Wall and the worldwide fame of Russian dissidents such as the writer Alexander Solzhenitsyn and the scientist Andrei Sakharov. Courageous individuals like these started a ripple effect which gathered momentum and hastened the decline of communism throughout Eastern Europe. Winston Smith can be seen as a forerunner.

QUESTIONS & ANSWERS

The essay topics below show a range of possible styles and formats, and are suitable for senior English assessment tasks and examinations.

Essay topics

1 'Winston's fate is inevitable from the beginning of the story.'

How far do you agree?

2 "He felt as though he were wandering in the forests of the sea bottom, lost in a monstrous world where he himself was the monster. He was alone."

Why does Winston feel this way?

3 'Despite Winston's ultimate fate, the courage he displays is inspiring.'

How far do you agree?

4 'Winston's desperate need to form connections with other people is the cause of his downfall.'

Discuss.

5 'Though we despise O'Brien's cruelty, we find him a fascinating character.'

How far do you agree?

6 'The proles of Oceania, with their passive acceptance of their lot in life, are happier than those, like Winston, who try to rebel.'

How far do you agree?

7 'The novel shows us that the individual will always be at the mercy of the state.'

Discuss.

8 'The novel suggests that an accurate understanding of the past is necessary both to the individual and to the wider community.'

Discuss.

9 'The novel shows that fear is the chief weapon used by those in power.'

Discuss.

10 'The novel shows that the manipulation of language is the most powerful means of controlling the minds of individuals.'

Discuss.

11 'The novel shows that, even in the midst of tyranny, admirable human qualities can survive.'

Discuss.

12 'The novel shows that the need for human relationships is the most powerful of human needs.'

Discuss.

Analysing a sample topic

'The novel suggests that an accurate understanding of the past is necessary both to the individual and to the wider community.' Discuss.

A possible approach to this topic

- Highlight the key terms in the statement: *accurate understanding of the past, necessary, the individual* and *the wider community*.
- Formulate your contention in relation to the statement. Remember that you are not required to simply agree with it, unless it seems appropriate to do so.
- Modify the statement so that it reflects your own viewpoint.
- Gather together your material under brief, clear headings, such as the following.

Accurate understanding of the past

- Show how this is prevented by the Party.
- Include examples of the Party's falsification of history.
- Show the effects of this on the citizens of Oceania.

The individual

- Illustrate the importance of the past to Winston.
- Show Winston's need to make sense of his own life.

The wider community

- Illustrate the importance of an accurate sense of history.
- Discuss the effects of the lack of a shared history, such as isolation, social divisions, and vulnerability to state control.

How to structure your essay

- You need to develop a consistent argument about the statement.
- Begin with a strong opening paragraph that telescopes down the main ideas you will develop later. The opening should be fairly general.
- In your subsequent paragraphs, work from the general to the specific. Work in plenty of detail from the text to illustrate your points. Blend short quotations in with your own words.
- In your final paragraph, strongly reiterate your main argument, but avoid repeating yourself. Ending with a relevant quotation can work well.
- Establish strong links between all the paragraphs of your essay. Use linking words and phrases; use a key word from the last sentence of one paragraph in the first sentence of the next.
- Good topic sentences signpost your main ideas and help you to stay on track. It is also wise to have one sentence in each paragraph that relates directly to the question.

SAMPLE ANSWER

'Winston's desperate need to form connections with other people is the cause of his downfall.' Discuss.

Winston Smith is indeed a man who suffers deeply from the loneliness he has been 'locked' into by the brutal regime under which he is forced to live. Under the rule of the Party, truly intimate relationships and the open exchange of ideas between people are prohibited. Like almost anyone, he has a strong need to feel connected to other people, but his problem is exacerbated because his rebellion makes him feel like an outsider in his rigidly conformist society. Winston's need to escape his loneliness certainly contributes largely to his terrible fate, but there are other contributing factors besides this.

Under the rule of the Party, the citizens of Oceania no longer have friends; instead they have 'comrades'. The mass rallies and other activities organised by the Party, in order to cement its control over the people, never offer any opportunity for genuine connection with others. Winston feels deep hostility towards Big Brother and the Party; his sense of isolation is exacerbated by these activities. Furthermore, the Party discourages normal family ties and, in particular, disapproves of sex, except for the purpose of procreation. Not even this purpose is considered entirely desirable, so that there are plans to introduce artificial insemination ('*artsem*') as an alternative to natural procreation. Winston's loneliness, then, is both intellectual – he has no one with whom to share his dissident thoughts – and sexual. His need to relieve both these forms of loneliness ultimately leads him to take the fatal risks of approaching O'Brien, in the hope that he will be sympathetic to his ideas, and of beginning his relationship with Julia, a relationship which is discovered by the Thought

Police. Winston has no real justification for believing that O'Brien is on his side; his pressing need to confide in another person leads him to persuade himself that O'Brien is sympathetic to him.

Winston's need for more intimate companionship draws him into his relationship with Julia. This is a particularly dangerous relationship since Julia is also a 'thought-criminal', deeply hostile to the Party. Renting the room above Mr Charrington's shop, in order to have a place to make love with Julia, is another risk that his need for intimacy drives him to take. The depth of his need seems to be a contributing factor in his misjudgement of Mr Charrington, a member of the Thought Police posing as a kindly old antique dealer.

It is not only the need for companionship and intimacy that dooms Winston, although it is important in sealing his fate. It is his deep integrity which finally drives him to become a dissident and to set his mind against Big Brother. He sees through the lies upon which the Party's rule is based, and he takes the ultimately fatal risk – by the end of the story we know he will be 'vaporized' – of expressing his opposition to those lies. In addition, he needs to discover the truth about his earlier, forgotten personal life and also about the life of the society as a whole. His action of approaching the old man to discover the truth about life before the Revolution is dangerous and will almost certainly be detected by the Thought Police.

Winston's downfall is largely due to his need for connection with others, but it is also his courage and integrity that leads him to set himself up as 'a minority of one'. The Thought Police judge his behaviour as 'insane' and imposed their drastic 'cure' upon him.

REFERENCES & READING

Text

Orwell, George 2000, *Nineteen Eighty-Four*, Penguin, London. First published in 1949.

Newspaper article

Atwood, Margaret 2003, 'Orwell and Me', *The Guardian*, 16 June, http://www.theguardian.com/books/2003/jun/16/georgeorwell.artsfeatures

Film

Nineteen Eighty-Four 1984, dir. Michael Radford, MGM. Starring John Hurt, Richard Burton and Suzanna Hamilton.

Other references

Booker, Christopher 2004, *The Seven Basic Plots: Why We Tell Stories*, Continuum, London.

Orwell, George 1981, *Animal Farm*, Penguin, Ringwood (1945).

Orwell, George 2000, *Essays*, Penguin, London.
Interesting essays include 'A Hanging', 'The Prevention of Literature' and 'Politics and the English Language'.

Shelden, Michael 1991, *Orwell: The Authorised Biography*, HarperCollins, New York.